Revealing Abba in the Psalms

Book 2: Psalms 42 through 72

By John A. Fazio

How Jesus saw God as Abba

info@thefaithtranslation.com
thefaithtranslation.com

John A. Fazio
967 Prescott Blvd
Deltona, FL 32738

ISBN 978-1-7358215-3-5

Table of Contents

Preface

A few things that you should know before reading "Revealing Abba".

The Psalms are from the very heart of God, Jesus, who is the exact expression of God's heart toward you. They reveal not only who God is but also who man is and has always been to Him. Jesus saw that Abba was with Him to Father His life and declared how He will also be with you to Father your life.

The Father shows us in Jesus an expected end, as I was with Jesus so will I be with you.

You will see that the verses are not numbered. I wanted readers to see and be focused on the heart of the Father for them and not on the word for word interpretation of verses. At one point I would have told you that these writings were not as technical as most of my other writings but today I am persuaded that seeing this was the Father's message from the beginning and Jesus' greatest ministry to reveal it to us, I would say in its simplicity, it is also very technical. The Psalms contain the entire gospel and heart of God for you. Read it often and be blessed.

You will also see that most verses end in a semi colon, this is because I believe each Psalm is a single thought.

Here is some terminology I would also like to address.

Innocence/innocent: When you see the word innocence or innocent, it is speaking about how even though man-kind was married to death, it could not be a word that they were not the children of God. And this charge was the very accusation the devil brought against Jesus, saying if you are the Son of God turn these stones into bread. Tempting Jesus to use His own strength to preserve His life. And again, this same accusation came while He was on the cross. In raising Jesus from the dead, we see in Romans 1:4 that God declared that He was the Son of God with power, justifying all men as innocent of the accusation that because of death they were not the sons and daughters of God.

Enemy/enemies: My concern with these terms is that one might think it refers to people. Let's be clear about two points we can see in scripture. 1. Death was God's enemy, 2. We do not wrestle against flesh and blood. Nor did Jesus' wrestle against flesh and blood. People are not our enemies.

Flesh/Flesh and Bone: Many have been taught that the flesh is bad. And certainly, to use the strength contained in your flesh to try and preserve your life would be by definition sin. And of course, Paul states in Corinthians that flesh and blood shall not inherit the kingdom of God. But when Jesus was raised from the dead and He appeared to His disciples and He said, touch me, for a spirit does not have flesh and bone as you see I do.

We see in Ezekiel 16 that God found man in his blood, corrupted/defiled by blood it says. And Leviticus says the strength of the flesh is in the blood. Herein lies the symbol of corruption and death. And we see that the testimony of Jesus is that He let His blood run out. And appeared from the grave, immortal, in a flesh and bone body that will never die again.

So, we can see in the physical resurrection that God does not see the flesh as evil. The flesh is neutral but to use your flesh to try and establish and preserve your life would be the way that leads to destruction.

But we have this treasure in earthen vessels, that the excellency of the power may be of God, and not of us. 2 Cor 4:7

Though we live in perishable bodies, by the power of God, the Spirit of God will these mortal bodies be quickened. And as Romans 6 says as we are in the likeness of His death so will we be in the likeness of His resurrection.

Perspective: The Psalms contain both thoughts and conversations between Jesus and the Father that prophetically came from David's heart. Most theologians would call only certain Psalms messianic Psalms, but I am fully persuaded that all the Psalms are messianic, to use their term.

Much of the perspective that I have written here is Jesus as high priest but even to be our high priest Jesus had to be and was a man. And seeing Jesus the man, and His words and thoughts to the Father as death begins to encircle Him and manifest in His body, reveal the faith, which is the persuasion in Jesus' heart that caused Him to not open His mouth to defend Himself but to simply cry out "Abba, into your hands do I commit My life".

And we see how Jesus as a man in flesh that could die, was persuaded to allow His flesh to rest in the hope He had from the Father to not leave Him in the grave or allow His body to see corruption but to raise

Him. A sure hope and an evidence we now have in the bodily resurrection of Jesus Christ.

Lastly, it is written from the perspective that we now know the end from the beginning. As Jesus also knew He would be raised up and spoke about it for over three and a half years of ministry, so do the Psalms and all the scriptures speak of the spirit of prophecy that is found in Jesus Christ; that is, His death, His burial, His resurrection, and ascension, as well as His return.

Grace and Peace,

John Fazio

Psalm 42

As a deer longs for a drink from the brook, so is My desire to share in Your life and You in Mine, O Abba.

I long for the day I will stand before You forever in glorified human flesh.

When I was sorrowful unto death; and the enemy surrounded Me saying; where is your God now?

I poured out My heart to You Abba and You strengthened Me; and I remembered the glory I had with You before the world was; and the joy that was set before Me; and I heard Your voice answer; saying;

Why are You cast down? O My Son; and why are You disturbed in Your spirit; hope in Me; Abba; for I will surely glorify and rescue Your life and seat You at My right hand;

O My Abba; though My life is cast down within Me; into Your hands do I trust My life;

Death has come upon Me to overtake Me; But You Abba will never leave or forsake Me;

For You Abba; directed Your loving-kindness to Me in the daytime; and You put a new song in My heart in the nighttime; O Abba; the shepherd of My life.

In My affliction I cried out to You Abba; And You heard My cry and delivered Me; from all the oppression of My enemy; death;

With a sword in My side My enemies did reproach Me; saying where is your God? You answered Me; Abba; saying;

Why are You cast down? O My Son; and why are You disturbed in Your spirit; hope in Me; Abba; for I will surely glorify and rescue Your life and seat You at My right hand.

Psalm 43

Judge Me O Abba; declaring My innocence; protect and defend My life from the adversary, death; and deliver Me from that which seeks to harm Me;

For You are My God and My strength O Abba; You will not cast Me away; or leave Me in sorrow; under the oppression of death;

Testify in Me of Your grace and truth; persuading all people of their inheritance; in beholding how, You raised Me up in an incorruptible human body and seated Me at Your right hand;

In the midst of My sorrow, You strengthen Me; turning My sadness into joy; and I rested; for when I cried out in My affliction, "Abba!" You answered Me; saying;

Why are You cast down? O My Son; and why are You disturbed in Your spirit; hope in Me; Abba; for I will surely glorify and rescue Your life and seat You at My right hand; forevermore.

Psalm 44

We have heard with our ears, O Abba, what You have spoken to Your children through the prophets, of all Your wonderful works;

Prophesying, how in Me; the strength of Your hand; You will destroy and cast out the enemy that has afflicted all the people;

For they did not possess the land by their own ability, neither did they save themselves by their own hand: but by Me, Your right arm; and the light of Your face to the world; and by Your favor and everlasting kindness were they delivered;

You are My King, O Abba; You testify in Me; the deliverance of all people;

Psalm 44

Let Us destroy the enemy; death, let Us declare Your name Abba; and testify how You trample underfoot, that which rises up against Me;

For I do not trust in My own strength; or My own ability to save Myself; but into Your hands do I commit My life Abba;

You save Me from death and put to shame and disarm that which sought to harm Me and all Your beloved;

In You Abba; do I boast all day long; and at Your right hand is praise and fullness of joy forever;

But in Your everlasting kindness did You reject man's union to death, of trusting in the strength of their hand for life; to fight in their own strength;

You turned away from that which made them barren; and from that which sought to destroy them;

You gave them over to their own way where they were eaten, like sheep killed for food; and scattered among the enemy;

To be destroyed at the hand of the enemy for no profit;

A reproach among men, to be mocked by all around; a laughingstock;

Their shame was always before them; causing them to cover their faces, perceiving all this as Your disapproval; But it was the voice of the enemy that cursed; and the enemy that sought to cause them harm;

All this has come upon Me; yet I have not forgotten Your truth Abba; but I ever trust in Your promise;

My heart is not moved; neither have My steps turned back from Your truth;

Though I am surrounded by the serpent and covered with the shadow of death;

I declare Your name O Abba; saying, into Your hands do I trust My life; not by strength of My own hand O Abba; or by any other name;

For You Abba search the heart; and have revealed the truth to man's heart in Me; In resting in You Abba and Your arm for life;

For I was counted as a sheep for the slaughter; persecuted, distressed and naked; saying;

Awake and hear My cry O Abba; save Me in My affliction;

Though it seemed You hid Your face for a moment; in everlasting kindness You delivered Me; testifying that You will never leave or forsake Me or Your beloved;

For though death surrounded Me and My life was bowed down to the dust of the earth; You saved Me Abba; and did not leave Me in the grave or allow Me to see corruption;

But You Abba delivered Me from death; and raised Me up in an immortal flesh and bone body; seating Me at Your right hand; declaring an eternal word and a certain hope to all people; that in Your everlasting kindness; You will also deliver those who rest in You for life; saving them from death and raising them unto the same life and immortality they see in Me.

Psalm 45

Abba's heart overflows with excitement of His good word; speaking and revealing in Me; the beauty He sees when He beholds the ones who He has made. My tongue is like the pen of a ready writer; to declare Abba's heart to all people;

Abba, You have bestowed upon Me; Your glory and honor; that the children of men might find their beauty in Me; The abundance of Your heart flows from My lips; and You have blessed Me forever;

You clothed Me with grace and truth; O Abba; with Your splendor and good opinion;

And in Your strength and not My own do I declare the truth; that in Me; will You destroy the enemy; and at Your right hand You shall show forth the incredible riches of their inheritance.

Your arrows of truth and judgment are a death blow to the corrupt wisdom of the enemy; that which has sought to destroy Your beloved;

You seat Me Abba at Your right hand in an incorruptible human body; forever and ever; establishing and declaring the truth about all people; and rightly judging their innocence;

Abba, You love that which brings life and hate that which destroys or harms Your beloved; therefore Abba; did You anoint Me with gladness above all My friends; and set that joy before Me; that We might bring it to pass;

Abba, You have clothed Me with a sweet aroma of myrrh, aloes and cinnamon; they fill My palaces; the chamber where I bring Your beloved;

I desire Your beloved as a bridegroom does his beautiful bride; to stand at My right hand decked out in gold;

Listen and consider My beloved; I have delivered you from your bondage; cast off the garment of captivity; and dwell in My house forevermore;

I have greatly desired your beauty; I am Your Lord; I want to serve you with My life. Showering you with gifts; whereby even the richest will see your favor;

Abba's glorious good opinion of you will clothe you with the same life and immortality you see in Me;

My bride is presented to Me; perfect and complete; in immortality; with rejoicing and gladness will she enter into My presence; kings and royal priests shall you be in the earth.

Abba has made My name to be remembered for all generations; a testimony for all people; therefore, shall the people praise You Abba; forever and ever.

Psalm 46

Abba is My refuge, My strength and My hope; My help and comfort from all calamity and affliction;

Therefore, I will not fear, though the world presses in on Me and all the things that are seen are shaken, and carried away to deep waters;

Though the waters rage and trouble surround Me; I am fully persuaded;

Abba is a river of life; and the streams of that river fill Me; the city of God; with joy and gladness; Abba's life and peace flood Me; the tabernacle of the most high;

Abba is always with Me and in Me; I will not be moved: He is constantly persuading My heart of His everlasting kindness toward Me; and all His beloved;

The enemy roars and the kingdoms are shaken; trying to speak a word of lack to Me and to all Abba's beloved; Abba has spoken an eternal word in Me; the sound of Abba's voice spoken in Me; destroys and dissolves the enemy in the earth;

For Abba has testified in Me; that He is with us; He is the Lord strong and mighty, testifying that the same life and immortality you behold in Me will also be revealed in you; your refuge and inheritance;

Come; behold in Me the works of Abba; how in Me; He destroyed all sin and death and that which sought to harm His beloved;

Abba's yoke is easy. He has ended the corrupt wisdom in the earth that caused men to struggle to give themselves life; by disarming and removing the sting of death; the life and immortality they behold in Me, overcomes and consumes it;

Stand still in awe and know that the word that Abba has spoken in Me; is a sure and eternal word about you; that word is far above all that is in the world, swallowing up any corrupt wisdom; bringing it to nothing;

For Abba has testified in Me; that He is with us; He is the Lord strong and mighty, testifying that the same life and immortality you behold in Me will also be revealed in you; your refuge and inheritance.

Psalm 47

All Your beloved Abba clap their hands and shout with great joy at the sound of Your voice; at the word You declare in Me; victory over death;

For You Abba are a great and awesome God and have set Me as King over all the earth; to subdue all things; for all people and nations; bringing all things under Our feet;

You have chosen Me Abba; as their inheritance before the foundation of the world; because of the beauty You behold in them; the apple of Your eyes; the ones You love;

Abba; You have seated Me at Your right hand; in Your life and immortality; declaring the victory over death;

Sing praises to Abba; sing praises unto our King; sing praises with understanding; for He has revealed in Me; His life and immortality;

Abba's wisdom reigns supreme; His testimony; in Me at His right hand; speaks a word to all people; of the life He has set apart for them;

That Abba has reconciled all things and all people back to Himself; He has highly exalted Me as a testimony; that you are His beloved child that He has promised to clothe with His life and immortality.

Psalm 48

Abba is great and the glory of His light shines in Me; the city of God; the place prepared and set apart for Him to dwell.

Beautiful is the height of that city and what delight Abba has in seating Me at his right hand; I am His joy and the joy of the whole earth; the dwelling place of the great King.

Abba has testified to the hearts of His beloved in Me; that He has always desired to come and seat them on high at His right hand;

Psalm 48

For all the kings of the world and its wisdom were assembled against Me; they passed by together.

They saw the brightness of My rising and they marveled; and they were troubled and distressed in heart and they took flight seeing their inability to give themselves life;

Fear took hold of them; distress and pain in their hearts as a woman in labor;

Behold Abba has broken the power of death and brought life and immortality to light in Me;

You have heard, and have seen the testimony of Abba in Me; that by seating Me in a glorified human body at His right hand; He has revealed that He has always desired to join Himself to you and seat you; His beloved; at His right hand;

Abba has established; and has declared His desire in Me; to come and joined Himself in perfect union to you; His dwelling place forever;

The loving-kindness of Abba that was revealed in Me has come to dwell in the hearts of His beloved; His holy temple;

According to Your name; O Abba; does Your light shine to the ends of the earth; in Me; Your right hand; that destroyed sin and death and all that sought to harm Your beloved.

Let all people and all nations rejoice; and Your sons and daughters be glad because of Your righteous judgments; to declare their innocence and bring to nothing that which could harm them.

Behold how in Me; Abba has spoken a word about the beauty He sees in you; declaring the glorious, good opinion He has of you;

Remember how He has destroyed sin and death; and seated you at His right hand; as a co-heir and co-sharer of His life forever; declaring an eternal word to all people and generations;

For this God is our Abba forever and ever; He has testified in Me that He has conquered death and given His life and immortality as an inheritance.

Psalm 49

Hear the voice of your Abba in Me; all you people; Listen closely; all you inhabitants of the world;

Both those who see their inability; and those who trust in their own strength to give themselves life; whether they be rich or poor; together.

Psalm 49

My mouth declares the wisdom and the heart of Abba; that He is the protector and defender of My life and the life of His beloved; and the meditation of Abba's heart gives understanding that He will never leave or forsake Me or allow Me to see corruption.

In parables, I utter things which have been kept secret from the foundation of the world.

Why then would I fear in the day when death tries to tell Me that I lack the life of a son; when the corrupt wisdom of the world attempts to entice Me to enlist My own ability to save Myself?

Those who trust in themselves; boast in their own strength for life; and in the multitude of things they can obtain by their own efforts.

None of them can by their own ability or substance raise themselves from death; nor can they provide the offering that could save their brother from death.

For the redemption of their life is precious, and of such value that it can only be found in Me; the Word made flesh; and in the incorruptible life you see in Me seated at Abba's right hand in an immortal flesh and bone body forever;

The abundance of perishable things can never produce the life that Abba desires to give you; nor can it keep you from the grave and corruption;

For you see that both wise and foolish men die; and leave their substance to others;

In their hearts they say and believe that their houses and substance will continue forever to all generations; they trust in that which they have built with their own hands and their own name;

Nevertheless, the way that seems right to them will destroy them; those who trust in it like beasts will perish;

Their way is foolishness; yet for generations their descendants have ignorantly believed the same;

Like sheep they have been led to be slaughtered; death has been their guide; but I am the good shepherd and Abba has given Me dominion over all flesh to consume death and the grave of its power;

Abba is My shepherd and redeems My life from death; not allowing Me to see corruption; receiving Me unto Himself and seating Me at His right hand;

Abba has testified in Me; that you do not need be afraid when you see death and it tries to tell you; you lack what you need for life; or when you see the increase of those trusting in themselves for life;

For those things will all perish; and will all see corruption;

For though while a man lives, he tries to build a good report of his life through the abundance of things; and other men sing his praises; trusting in this way leads to death and corruption; just as it did for his ancestors;

For there is only incorruptible life found in Abba; and Abba has declared your sure testimony in Me; by raising Me up in an immortal flesh and bone body and seating Me at His right hand;

But a man that is trying to serve himself life through corruptible things; does not see or understand the wisdom that Abba has revealed in Me; and is like a beast that will perish.

Psalm 50

Abba; is a mighty God; even the Lord; who has spoken over the earth from the beginning; calling for all things to be gathered unto Himself;

Abba's light has shined out of Me; His dwelling place; and has shown forth the beauty and perfection He sees in Me and His beloved;

Abba comes declaring the truth in Me; and like a fire it devours and swallows up all things contrary to His life; and like a whirlwind sweep them away;

He has declared from the heavens above and unto the earth, the innocence of His people;

Abba has always desired to gather His beloved unto Himself; those who see the Word of their testimony in My face;

And Abba declares from heaven, in Me at His right hand, that He has destroyed death, raising Me from the grave in immortal flesh and bone, and seating Me at His right hand: and in Me has Abba declared that death and the grave have lost their sting;

Hear Abba! for He has spoken a word to Me and in Me; testifying that I can trust Him with My life; to save Me from death and give Me His life as a gift; declaring, I AM God, even Your Abba who gives You My life;

I will not correct you for your many offerings when they are born from the joy of seeing the life I have promised you from the beginning;

But it has never been My desire to take bulls and goats from your house or your table. I don't need them. All the beasts of the earth are mine, I own them all;

If I were hungry I would not ask you; because the earth is Mine and everything in it if that is what I desired;

Do you think I feast on bulls and drink the blood of goats?

Rather, I have waited with great anticipation for Your offering of joy and thanksgiving; and seeing it overflow in Your heart toward Me when You behold My testimony; fully persuaded of the promise to save You from death and corruption and give You My life. This is the offering I have truly desired from the beginning;

And in the day of trouble, You cried out to Me; "Abba" and I delivered You and You glorified Me;

But to those who labor and toil to give themselves life; Abba says, apart from Me, what could you ever do to produce My life? Or that the fruit of your mouth would ever glorify Me;

Seeing you rejected My life as a gift; you discard My words behind you;

When you saw the thief who takes men's lives and puts them in bondage, you conspired with him; and became a partaker with those who run after false gods;

Your mouth heaps hardships on men too hard to bear; and your tongue speaks lies about Abba and man;

You sit and speak against your brother; the son of man; and you slander your own mother's son.

All these things you have said and done darkening My council and I was silent; you even thought that I was just like you; but I will declare My testimony before your eyes; admonishing and setting everything in order; reconciling all things back to Myself;

Consider My Testimony, you that have forgotten the promise of Abba to give you His life as a gift; lest destruction from upon you; for there is no one else who can deliver you but Abba;

Whosoever offers perfect praise, glorifies Abba; calling upon His name; bringing the offering He has always desired: when you see Me offering thanksgiving to Abba; in fulfillment of the life Abba has promised from the beginning; It declares to you the salvation of Abba and His incorruptible life as your inheritance.

Psalm 51

O Abba; You are merciful and gracious unto Your beloved according to Your loving-kindness: Let Us show forth the abundance of Your goodness, truth and tender mercy; blotting out the way that brings the fruit of death which is contrary to Your life;

Purging their hearts from the world's wisdom and removing the death reigning over them;

For the fruit of death manifesting in them from the corrupt wisdom they have believed on is ever before them;

Against Your truth Abba have they believed; going contrary; they were not partaking of Your life; this way brought hardships and death upon them;

O that they would see that way only brings death; so that they may clearly see Your judgment and be persuaded of the word You have spoken in Me: Your judgment of their innocence and of Your blessing and life as a gift.

Behold, I was formed inside of a world filled with corruptness and darkness; and My mother did conceive Me in a world where death was reigning over man.

Behold, You Abba desired to reveal the truth to Me and in Me; and were ever influencing My heart; nurturing and making known to Me Your wisdom;

I delight to do Your will Abba; to bear their death in My body and purge their conscience with My blood; declaring their innocence and washing their slate clean;

You lay before Me the joy and gladness of hearing those who have been under the crushing weight of sin and death as they rejoice in seeing their testimony in Me;

Putting an end to that union which served them with death; blotting out all that is contrary to Your wisdom and Your way unto life;

That they might behold in Me; a new creation; and see their innocence; O Abba, and be born from the Spirit of life;

You have testified in Me; that in bearing their sin in My body, You never cast Me away from Your presence; or removed Your Spirit from Me;

But rather You restored Me to the glory I had with You before the world was; and have seated Me at Your right hand in an immortal human body; testifying how in trusting You with My life; You saved Me from death and upheld Me with Your incorruptible life;

Now, I have spoken a word to all those experiencing the fruit of death; teaching them Your ways; and those who were not partaking of Your life can see Your life as their inheritance;

Removing all guilt and shame; O Abba, You delivered Your beloved from the sting of death; and all that sought to bring them harm;

O Abba; You opened My lips and I have declared Your name in the earth; and Your good opinion of man;

For You Abba never desired sacrifice or burnt offerings because it could never satisfy Your hope for Your life with man;

Rather, Your longing desire was that in man seeing their inability to give themselves life; they could behold in Me Your desire and ability to give them Your life as a gift; O Abba; this is the only sacrifice that could ever satisfy Your hearts desired;

It was Your good pleasure; to reveal in Me, Your desire to share Your life eternally with Your beloved: Let Us make our abode with them forever;

Then will You be pleased Abba, with the sacrifice and offering that destroyed death and all that was against Your beloved; and gave them Your life as an inheritance; then will they call upon Your name; rejoicing in their hearts; in the certain hope that they can trust You Abba with their life.

Psalm 52

Why do you trust in and boast in the strength of your own hand to save you from death; O mighty man? It is Abba who will preserve and protect your life; His everlasting kindness endures forever;

Your tongue spews perverse things; from the corrupt wisdom that has pierced your heart; working deceit that leads to destruction;

You love the life you can serve yourself more than the goodness of Abba and His ability to save you from death and serve you with His life;

You love the way unto death; O you perverted wisdom;

Abba will destroy you forever; plucking you up by the roots from your dwelling; dying away the death you have brought upon His beloved in the earth;

Those who see how in Me Abba has destroyed death and given His life will stand in awe and rejoice;

Behold also how the man who made not God his strength but trusted in the fruit he could produce and accumulate by his own hands; has only death reigning over him; how trying to strengthen himself led to his own destruction;

Behold I am your inheritance; His anointed; seated at Abba's right hand; as a man in the beauty and immortality which Abba has promised from the beginning; Behold, I trust in the mercy and everlasting kindness of Abba forever and ever;

My testimony will forever speak a word of what Abba has done; to deliver Me from death; and how I harkened diligently to and trusted in His promise, for all those partaking of His life to behold and rest in Abba's promise of the same incorruptible life in them.

Psalm 53

The fool labors to preserve his own life, saying in his heart that there is no one and most certainty not God to serve me with life, so I must serve myself; this corrupt wisdom does not allow their heart to rest in You and Your life, Abba.

You look down from heaven upon Your beloved, longing for them to understand Your everlasting kindness toward them; and Your desire to share Your life with them; so that they might look to You for the life their heart has always longed for;

Every one of them has turned away from Your way that leads to life; they all have corruption and death reigning over them; there is none that rests in You and Your ability to give them life, no, not one;

Have all those laboring to preserve their life not seen it is the way which leads to death? They lay burdens too hard to bear on those who see they cannot ever serve themselves the life they truly desire; not acknowledging it is only found in You, Abba;

There is no rest in this corrupt way of thinking but only torment; Abba has brought rest in Me; bringing destruction upon all that which was against you; putting it to shame; Abba has despised the way that brought death to His beloved;

O that all might see their salvation and inheritance in Me; Your dwelling place and Your word made immortal flesh; for In Me, Abba, You have rescued Your people from the bondage of death where all can find rest in You and rejoice and be glad.

Psalm 54

Deliver Me, O Abba; testifying in Me of Your name and Your strength;

Psalm 54

Hear My prayer, O Abba; give ear to Me, that all might hear the words of My mouth;

For those who have turned aside from Your way unto life have come against Me; tempting Me to trust in My ability, seeking to destroy My life; they do not see You are the only way unto life;

Behold, My testimony declares that You Abba are My helper and My deliverer; You uphold Me, upholding My life, setting Me at Your right hand; giving sure hope to all who see Your promise of life made immortal flesh in Me;

Abba Your truth will destroy the way unto death; bringing it to nothing, cutting it off from the earth;

For the joy set before Me, I will freely do your will O Abba, offering the sacrifice You have desired from the foundation of the world; so that all might rest in You; partaking of Your incorruptible life as their inheritance;

For You Abba, have delivered Me out of all adversity; destroying the enemy; death; and all that was against Me; bringing to light in Me, the desire of Your heart for all Your beloved.

Psalm 55

O Abba You hear My prayer and hide not Your face from Me in My affliction;

You attend unto Me and hear Me when I cry: I groan loudly in My trouble;

Because death has crept up on Me trying to tell Me I lack Your life; I am persecuted and pressed in by those who reject Your ways; they accuse Me of using evil to do good; tempting Me to save Myself; and in anger they hate Me;

My heart bears the pain of those who have all their lives been subjected to the terrors of death; they have fallen upon Me;

This fear of death has tried to come upon Me and cover Me; to overwhelm Me; saying,

Who will give Me wings like a dove; so that I might take flight and be at rest? Only in You Abba, does My heart find rest, hiding Me safely from troubles; escaping the affliction of the enemies that have encamped around me;

Let Us destroy, O Abba; the corrupt wisdom that has caused violence and strife to dwell in the hearts of Your beloved;

Psalm 55

Day and night it torments them; trouble and sorrows fill their hearts;

Labor and toil are in the midst of them; It never departs from them; constantly speaking lies to their hearts;

For the ones who accuse and reject Me are not My enemies; if it was only the one who did magnify himself against Me; I would have just concealed Myself from him;

But it was man; My coequals, My friends, and My love ones;

We had sweet fellowship and intimate conversation as we walked in Your house together Abba;

Certainly, death has seized upon them, reigning over them; hardships and labor consume their conscience; and trouble follows them;

As for Me; I call upon You Abba and You rescue My life from death and corruption;

Morning, noon and night, I fellowship with You Abba and You always hear My voice when I cry out to You;

Delivering My soul from the corruption in this world; ministering peace to Me from all that comes against Me;

You hear Me Abba, and bring to nothing all that tried defiled Your image and likeness; You have reigned supreme from the beginning;

Those trusting in themselves for life refuse to change their minds; being blinded to Your goodness toward them; therefore, they do not trust You as Abba;

Rather they plot to kill Me and those resting in You for life; betraying My friendship and seeing Me as their enemy;

Their words are smooth and flattering but their hearts are deceived and set against Your way unto life Abba;

I trust My life to You Abba; Testifying that You will sustain Me; My life is contained in You; You will never allow Me to see corruption but will rather, save Me from death, raising Me up to sit at Your right hand forevermore;

And You O Abba will conquer death and all that seeks to destroy Your beloved; death and corruption will be swallowed up in immortality; though some will reject Your life and perish; I have trusted in You; speaking an eternal word, so that all flesh can go to rest in the certainty they will inherit the same glory and immortality revealed in Me.

Psalm 56

O Abba; You ever influence My heart that You can be trusted to preserve and protect My life from all harm; for scoffer's pant after Me seeking to trample Me; daily they press in to crush Me;

The enemy seeks to destroy Me; And daily brings accusation against Me; You, O Abba are the most high who brings grace and truth;

In My time of affliction; I trust in You.

O Abba; In the word You have spoken, that I am Your beloved Son, do I find My testimony and give praise; in You O Abba have I placed My trust; not fearing what flesh and blood can do to Me;

Every day they pervert My words; and the word that I am Your Son; all their thoughts are against Me and are defiled in believing the lie that they must clothe themselves with life;

They abide in their own way, to preserve their own lives; waiting for opportunity to take mine from Me;

Shall they escape death by this corrupted wisdom? In Your passion; O Abba; let Us triumph over and cast down this way that seeks to destroy Your beloved;

You; Abba testified in Me; how You saw My tears and heard My cry and recorded them for all to remember;

That when I cried to You, You heard Me in My affliction; conquering the sting of death; fully persuading Me that I can trust You with My life; that You Abba would never leave or forsake Me, but are always for Me;

In You Abba; I have spoken well of and declare Your word to all people; In Me Abba is Your grace and truth exalted and revealed;

In You Abba have I placed My trust; I am not afraid that man can do anything to harm My life; being fully persuaded of the indestructible life You have promised Me;

Testifying to all people; how You preserved and protected My life; not leaving Me in the grave to see corruption but raising Me up and seating Me at Your right hand in glory and immortality;

Your Joy rest upon Me; O Abba; I desire to do your will, the offering the You have longed for from the beginning; testifying in Me of the promise; to save Me and all your beloved from death and corruption; raising them to the same glory they behold in Me;

For in You having delivered Me from sin and death; and seating Me at Your right hand in an incorruptible flesh and bone body; have You declared how You can be trusted to also deliver all who place their trust in You; that they may walk with You Abba in the cool of the day in the same glory and immortality forevermore.

Psalm 57

Let Your mercy be upon Me; O Abba; ever persuading My heart of Your loving-kindness; for My heart has found its rest in You; trusting in You to preserve and defend My life until all affliction has passed;

I cry unto You Abba, the most high; for it is by strength of Your hand that all things are brought to perfection and completion;

You have sent Me into the world and saved Me from death and corruption and all that seeks to destroy Me and Your beloved; You sent Me; as a testimony for all people; declaring Your heart in grace and truth;

I dwell among hungry lions who fiercely seek their prey to stay alive; men, who in their lust for life through their own ability, labor and toil; seeking to take it by force;

Let Us exalt Your wisdom in the earth, above the heavens; O Abba; to give them Your life as a gift; Let Your good view and opinion of all Your beloved be proclaimed in Me;

The enemy has prepared a net that I might stumble at the truth; My soul is pressed in and brought low in My distress: they have dug a pit for Me; and by their own wisdom do they themselves fall into its trap;

My heart is fully persuaded of Your loving-kindness; O Abba: that life is only found in You; and out of My heart does My mouth speak; "into Your hands do I trust My life."

A new song have You put in My mouth, that all men may see it; declaring and speaking well of Your ability to save Me from death;

Awake to Abba's inheritance for you, in seeing the glory revealed in Me; awake and see in Me, how it is Abba who will save you and give you His life as a gift; raising You up to the same glory and immortality;

I declare this word from Your heart; O Abba; I sing it unto all people and all nations;

For Your loving-kindness for all people; that was testified in saving Me from death and raising Me to glory and immortality; is great in influencing men's heart of Your truth; that You have given them the promise of this same incorruptible life as a gift;

Let Your wisdom be exalted; O Abba; above the heavens; Let the glory and immortality You revealed in Me be above any word in all the earth.

Psalm 58

If you indeed want to speak of the justice of Abba; O congregation, instead of distorting it; see how it is revealed in Me; how that Abba has only ever wanted to come and destroy the death that was reigning over you and give you His life as a gift; otherwise, are you really judging correctly; O you sons of men?

For your heart and conscience are filled with labor and toil for life unto destruction; you conclude you are orphaned in the earth and must take it by force;

Those who labor and toil for life, feel separated from the life of Abba; as soon as that lie gives birth in their heart, they go astray;

This lie is born from the father of lies, the serpent; that snake whose corrupt wisdom has been planted in the earth; hardening men's hearts from hearing the truth;

You cannot overcome it in your own strength; even with cunning skill and eloquent speech, the wisdom of man can never subdue its power;

O Abba, let Us break the power and the sting of death; tearing down the way that leads to destruction;

Let all that seeks to destroy Your beloved fade away in an instant and be brought to nothing; circumcising their heart from the poison of the serpent;

Like a snail that melts away, so all that is contrary to My beloved will disintegrate, never to rise up again;

Before you can feel the sting of death, Abba shall take it away in a whirlwind; in His passion, He will utterly destroy death and all that might bring harm to His children;

All those who trust that it is Abba who will come to take vengeance on death and all that is against His beloved, shall rejoice; He shall trample over death; bringing an end to it in Me;

So that all men can behold and say; surely there is a reward for those who trust in Abba to save them from death and bring forth the very same life they see in Me, in them; certainly Abba is the One who will restore all things in the earth, removing every remnant of sin and death.

Psalm 59

Deliver Me from My enemies O My Abba: defend Me from all that would rise up against Me;

Deliver Me from the schemes of those who are trusting in their works, who with violence try to preserve the life of their flesh;

For they are just waiting to ambush Me and take My life; powerful men in the flesh, they seek to kill me though I have done them no harm;

They are quick to shed My blood though they find no guilt in Me; Awake to save Me Abba, and behold;

It is You Abba; The Lord God My defender; the giver of life; who will deliver Me from the enemy; and My life from the grave; and will visit all people and all nations with Your justice: taking vengeance and having no pity on death and upon that which served them with the fruit of death;

They return at evening barking out threats and going about the city;

Insults pour out of their mouths; they mock Me with their lips; saying, who will save you now?

But You Abba; laugh, knowing how You will deliver Me and come and destroy the death that they are experiencing;

It is by strength of Your hand Abba that I will be delivered; for You are My defense;

You Abba are the God of everlasting kindness, You will not allow Me to see corruption; visiting thousands with Your goodness and truth; In Me shall they see Your desire upon the enemy, death;

You slay them not; but give them over to what is in their heart; that they might see and not forget what is causing them to suffer; O Abba My deliverer;

For in the corruption of their mouth and the cursing of their lips, they allow themselves to be taken with pride; bringing them to a fall;

Consume them in Your passion to give them Your life; consume them with Your Spirit; that they may not perish; but that all would know that Your wisdom Abba rules over all and is far above any in the earth;

And let them return at evening; give them up to murmuring and make noise all around the city.

Psalm 60

Give them over to labor to have life by their own strength; and to looking to the world to find their food for life that they may see that it never satisfies;

But I will sing of Your strength Abba; I will tell of Your everlasting kindness; speaking an eternal word for all people and all nations; for You Abba are My defense and My refuge against the day when the death in the world tried to tell Me I lacked life;

In You O Abba, My strength; does My life and immortality at Your right hand proclaim to all people that You will also defend and preserve their life; O Abba, You are the God of everlasting kindness.

Psalm 60

O Abba, You have rejected the works of man's hands; because it is the way which brings destruction upon them to Your displeasure; O Abba, let Us reconcile them back to You.

You have shaken the foundations of the world; breaking it to pieces: heal the hearts of Your people; for they are afflicted;

You have shown them hard things; so that they might stand in awe of the works of Your hands and not their own; so that they might drink of the Word of life; and not destruction;

You have given Me; as a sign to those who place their trust in You Abba;

You have given an eternal word to them that worship You; that in Me, the only truth about them would be on display; the work You will do to deliver them from death; Selah;

So that Your beloved may be delivered from death; saved by Your right hand; by hearing the Word You have declared in My resurrection.

I rejoice Abba, that in Me, have You promised to give them Your life as an inheritance;

And that the glory they see in Me will utterly destroy any word that the world could speak about them; And they will be strengthened with the hope revealed in Me; Abba's teaching and instruction unto life;

This word washes men's heart clean from trusting in the works of their own hands; bringing peace and rest in seeing the work of Abba to conquer death and give them His life in Me;

Who will bring Me into the strong city? Who can save Me from this body of death and give Me new life?

It is You O Abba; who has shown us that the works of our own hands bring death and destruction; but the works of Your hand will deliver us from death and give us life;

Only You Abba have the words of eternal life; the word that the world gives is emptiness and death;

But through the word that You have spoken in Me, Abba, will men receive strength, when they see how You have destroyed the enemy, death.

Psalm 61

O Abba, You heard Me when I cried, inclining unto Me in My affliction.

From the ends of the earth have I cried to You; and when My heart was overwhelmed, and death was pressing in on Me; You saved Me lifting Me up to glory and immortality at Your right hand;

For You Abba are My dwelling place and I am Yours; You protected Me from the enemy; death;

When I cried Abba, into Your hands do I trust My life; You clothed Me with Your life and immortality forever;

For You Abba, have heard Me and in Me; did You fulfill Your promise of eternal life; the thing You have desired for all men; and You have given Me an inheritance;

that all can behold and trust in the certainty of the same;

You have set Me as King to reign in righteousness; forever; declaring the justice of God; a life without end;

I will abide at Your right hand forever Abba; in grace and truth; and everlasting life; which You promised and prepared before the world began;

I will sing and praise Your name forever Abba; for My life at Your right hand is a living word, testifying to all who call upon Your name, the certainty of the same life they see in Me, which You have promised them from the beginning.

Psalm 62

With certainty do I rest in You Abba who preserves and protects My life; for I am fully persuaded that life and immortality are only found in You;

You are My strength and salvation from all that seeks to destroy My life; a foundation that is not moved by the word death has tried to speak to Me;

O death how long do you think you can attack man? You shall be slain, all of you, like a tottering fence you will fall;

Psalm 62

Those taken captive by you have consulted to keep Me from being exalted; they delight in lies; they speak flattering things to My face but in secret they slander My name;

Into Your hands do I trust My life Abba; for in You is where I find My confident expectation of life;

You are My strength and salvation from all that seeks to destroy My life; A foundation that is not moved by the word death has tried to speak to Me;

In You alone Abba will I find salvation from death and corruption and be exalted to Your right hand; You are My strength and My safety Abba;

Let Us speak a word to all people that they can trust You Abba with their life seeing their testimony in You delivering Me from the grave;

Certainly, the sons of men have no ability to give themselves life; and men who think more highly than they ought, tell lies; leaving you with empty promises;

Trust not in them who will oppress you, or lust after life in your strength; laboring and toiling in vain; if riches come to you, don't set your heart upon them;

Abba has spoken once in Me; listen and keep on hearing these things; knowing that your salvation comes by strength of His hand;

And unto Abba does goodness and kindness belong; giving to every man whose heart is persuaded by the word He has spoken in Me; the same life and immortality at His right hand.

Psalm 63

O Abba, You are My God; You are My desire day by day. My flesh longs to drink of Your incorruptible life in a dry land filled with death and corruption;

To see Your power and Your glory revealed in Me; inside of human flesh; with the glory I had with You before the world;

For Your loving-kindness is far above the life and the suffering of this present world; My lips continually speak well of You Abba;

In declaring Your name Abba and speaking of Your eternal life; will I magnify the strength of Your hand and Your name, forevermore;

My soul is only satisfied with the incorruptible word of Your life Abba; it nourishes and strengthens Me and all those who see it declared in Me; with overflowing joy do I only speak Your heart from My lips;

When I remember You and Your promise to give Me Your life; My heart is fully persuaded day and night;

Because, You are My helper and My deliverer; by strength of Your hand will I be delivered from death and corruption and will I rejoice;

My life is in You Abba and You in Me; at Your right hand do You hold Me forevermore;

But the enemy who seeks to destroy My life; will perish; and those who reject Your life Abba, will bring destruction upon themselves by the very sword that they wield, being devoured by the iniquity in their heart;

But I do rejoice, trusting You Abba with My life; speaking an eternal word to all people; that You will reveal in them, the same glory they see in Me, being raised up from the dead and seated at Your right hand in glorified human flesh and bone; triumphing over death and putting an end to the lies that it brought.

Psalm 64

O Abba, You hear Me cry in My affliction; Your life delivers Me from the fear of death;

Keeping Me safe from the word that I lack life; and from the crowd animated by the corrupt thinking death brings;

Those under the reign of death sharpen their tongues like a sword; to shoot their bitter words like arrows;

Waiting for an opportunity to ambush the righteous; they strike with no regard for man or God;

Conspiring together to bring misery; setting snares in secret, in hopes they surprise their victim;

They search to destroy the just; accomplishing it through false witness; revealing the exceedingly deep corruption that death has brought to their minds;

But You Abba, will destroy death with one arrow; suddenly slaughtering it with one blow;

So shall the way that animated the unjust collapse upon itself; all that see it will flee;

All those who see and believe the work that Abba has declared in Me to destroy death; shall consider themselves also risen together with Me;

The ones who see how Abba has rescued them from death and given them His life; the same life they see in

Me, will rejoice and be glad; trusting Him to bring forth the same glory and immortality in them.

Psalm 65

Perfect praise waits for You, O Abba, in Me, Your holy place; and unto You have I placed My trust; calling upon Your name before the congregation;

You heard Me when I called; O Abba; and unto You shall all be gathered together;

Though the wisdom of the world stands against Me; You Abba will triumph over it; destroying its wisdom and conquering death;

Blessed is the man who hears Me, Your word of eternal life and it causes him to approach You being fully persuaded of Your everlasting love and kindness; that he might dwell in You and You in him: he shall be satisfied with the goodness of Your house Abba; and he shall be Your holy temple.

By awesome works of righteousness; saving My life from the grave and corruption; have You answered O Abba, My salvation; providing a confident hope to all people near and far;

By Your strength Abba have I been seated at Your right hand with power in My resurrection;

Which word is able to quiet the hearts of those who were under the sway of death and the groaning of the people;

Those also who have dwelt in fear can see Your judgement and rejoice;

You Abba have visited the earth, watering it with Your word made flesh in Me; greatly blessing all who drink; a river of living water that springs into everlasting life; You prepared and provided My body as their food for life;

You rain abundantly on those of high and low degree; softening soil of their hearts and bringing forth a harvest;

You surround the year with Your goodness; and Your paths drip with the abundance of Your life;

Dripping even on dry land and bringing forth fruit and green leaves; all the hills of the earth rejoice on every side.

The pastures are clothed with large flocks; the valleys also are covered over with corn and grain; all are at rest and abundantly satisfied with Your goodness, they sing forth Your praises and declare Your goodness Abba.

Psalm 66

May all people and all nations shout for joy unto You Abba;

Singing forth as they behold the abundance and the fullness of Your glory revealed in Me; You have spoken most eloquently of Your good opinion of them, making their praise and thanksgiving perfect;

Let all see and say unto You Abba; How awesome are Your works; through Your power to conquer death; have You subdued all the ways that stand contrary to Your teaching and instruction unto life;

So that all the nations of the earth can be gathered unto You; singing to You, calling upon Your name;

Come and behold in Me the work that Abba has done to gather the children of men unto Himself;

Just as Abba turned the sea into dry land; so that the children of Israel went through on foot; do we also rejoice in Abba delivering us from death;

He has set Me at His right hand to rule forever; His eyes have always been upon all people; the just and the unjust; and those who reject Him trusting in themselves shall not be exalted;

All blessing and life come from You Abba; sing His praise all you people; and declare His goodness to all who will hear it;

You alone are the giver of life and You will not leave Me in the grave or allow Me to see corruption;

So that You O Abba might refine the hearts of Your beloved; to trust in You and not themselves;

Though death brought them into bondage; and laid affliction upon them;

Trampling, abusing and making slaves of Your beloved; In Me Abba have You brought them out, revealing that life and immortality are only found in You;

I go into Your presence with My blood; declaring You are the only source of the life revealed in Me, in My resurrection;

Which My lips have spoken in crying out to You in My affliction;

This is the finest and best offering that Your heart Abba has always desired; a sweet-smelling fragrance unto You; that all might call upon Your name and live;

Psalm 67

May all come and hear what You have done to rescue My life from the grave and set Me at Your right hand;

I cried unto You in My affliction and worshiped You with My tongue;

If I had exalted My own ability to save Myself from death, I would have never cried out for all to hear;

But I did cry out, and Abba heard Me; and He has answered by raising Me up to glory and immortality in My resurrection;

Blessing, glory and honor unto You Abba; You never turned away from Me but You heard My prayer, saving Me in My affliction; nor have You ever wavered from the hope of the everlasting life and immortality You had for Me and all Your beloved.

Psalm 67

O Abba, You are merciful to Me, and all Your beloved; You have spoken in Me with the highest speech and with great and precious promises of Your life; let Your face shine upon Me with adoration and acceptance;

Testifying of Your way unto life upon the earth; that salvation from death and corruption is revealed in Me, in My resurrection, for all people and all nations to behold;

Let all see Your life and immortality manifest in Me, let them call upon Your name Abba; let all people call upon You with perfect praise;

O let all people find a new song of joy in their heart; for You Abba have judged them as Your very own; not willing that any should perish but persuading them of Your sure promise of life in Me; the way unto life for all people and nations;

Let all see Your life and immortality manifest in Me, let them call upon Your name Abba; let all people call upon You with perfect praise;

Then Abba, shall the hope of Your life revealed in Me bring forth a harvest in the earth; that will bring many sons to glory; blessing them with Your incorruptible life;

Abba, You have spoken a sure word in Me; that all those who call upon Your name shall be saved from death and corruption; so that all the earth might see Your great works and stand in awe of You.

Psalm 68

Let Your Holy name be exalted as the only source of life Abba, when I arise in Your glory and immortality; conquering death in human flesh; scattering all Your enemies, let the enemies that despise You and molest Your beloved flee from before You;

As smoke is driven away as a mist, so drive away all that could harm Your beloved Abba; as wax melts before fire; so let death and the way that causes men's hearts to labor and toil for life perish at Your presence Abba; the One who serves us with life;

Let those who see their inability to give themselves life cry out to You, and be glad and delight, seeing the life You came to freely give them made immortal flesh in Me. Abba, let them rejoice before You forever; seeing the life their hearts have always longed for with joy that exceeds all they could ask or imagine;

Let our hearts make music and sing of Your name Abba; seeing the life You have exalted Me to at Your right hand; there is none like You Abba; the One who was, who is and who is to come; rejoicing is before You;

A Father to orphans, a defender of the widow and of all those who are alone and without strength in the earth; You Abba, are all those things in Me, Your holy habitation;

Abba You have set Me a Son over My own house; wherein all can dwell in Your life and love; giving liberty to those who were bound by death; but the ones who reject Your life dwell in a scorched and dry land;

O Abba, when You sent Me before the people, when You did march through the wilderness;

The earth trembled in awe and the heavens dripped of Your goodness; even the mountains acknowledged Your presence Abba; the God of all Your people;

You O Abba, sent Me to rain on them abundantly, confirming the promise of Your inheritance; even in their weakness;

Your life abides in Me; O Abba, wherein You have prepared Your goodness to those who are without strength;

Abba has spoken a word in Me; the Lord; the Word of life; and great are the number of those who hear it and declare the abundance of Your life;

All the princes and powers of this world did flee; and those who find their rest in My house; shall share in My inheritance;

Though you were laid down in the sheepfold to be slaughtered; yet now you gleam like a dove with wings of silver and gold;

Psalm 68

When Abba spoke in Me, the kings of the earth that tried to tarnish man's image scattered; and He washed His beloved white as snow;

I am the high hill wherein Abba dwells, a high hill as a hill with many peaks, where in You Abba desire to dwell;

Why leap you for joy, you high hills? Because you are His beloved; the hill that Abba desires to live in forever;

Abba, I am Your chariot; gathering twenty thousand, even thousands upon thousands; to dwell among them; a high hill set apart for You;

You Abba have seated Me on high, at Your right hand; leading those who were all their lives held captive to death and the fear of death to freedom; gathering them unto Yourself; and I have received gifts for all men; yes, even for the rebellious that You Abba; the One who is, who was and who is to come; might dwell among them;

Speak well of Abba; who has spoken well of you in Me, the Word of life; that conquered death; and day by day can persuade your heart of the life and immortality He revealed in Me;

Abba, is the giver of life; and the One who has served you with His life in Me; and unto Me has He given the keys of death and the grave;

And Abba has crushed the head of His enemy, death; and destroyed the reasoning of the one that continues to reject His life for the life they can give themselves;

Abba said, let Us renew them again unto life; wherein I will declare they are My children; pulling them from depths of darkness and death that was against them;

O Abba that We might take death away for all, leaving it in the grave; shutting the mouth of the accuser;

They have seen Your works; O Abba; even the work You performed in Me; Abba My King; when I declared Your name before the great congregation;

The singers went before Me; announcing My coming; the players followed after playing tambourine; like a bride seeing the coming of their groom, with great joy;

Speak well of Abba, who has spoken well of You; even in Me; declaring before the congregation that Abba was the only source of life and immortality;

All who find their testimony in Me, the Son; the testimony wherein all sin and death are subject; shall in the day of affliction find the same praise on their lips; whereby they call upon Your name Abba; and do no work but rest in You being exalted to Your right hand;

Abba has promised and declared that by strength of Me, His right hand, will you receive strength; and be exalted to glory and immortality; which He has promised since before the world began; and brought to light in Me;

Because You Abba have set Me, the Son over My own house wherein all can dwell in the complete fullness of Your life; shall kings call upon Your name; in the highest praise;

Rebuke the way of those that ignore Your life Abba for the life their own hand can give them; giving them over to their own passion until the proud might find humility; You have scattered that which harms Your beloved;

Princes shall come out from darkness into Your light and life Abba; and those in dry lands will find living water to drink in Me;

Sing praises unto Abba; seeing the life He revealed in Me, all you kingdoms of the earth; O sing praises, calling on the name of the One who has conquered death with eternal life;

For Abba has exalted Me to sit in immortal flesh at His right hand in the heavens; which were of old; declaring the Word that was from the beginning; with power according to the spirit of holiness; the life He set apart for us and made immortal flesh in My resurrection from the dead;

All glory and strength belongs to Him; who has strengthened Me; at His right hand in the heavens; that His strength might dwell in all;

O Abba, You are most awesome; revealing in Me the life You have always desired for Your beloved; to dwell with them forever; serving them with Your life, strength and power forevermore; Blessed be Abba in whom all blessings come.

Psalm 69

Save Me O Abba; in You alone do I trust to deliver Me; for troubles are come unto Me and My soul is sorrowful even unto death;

I am sinking deep into a pit where there is no way out; and the depths of the waters overflow Me;

I have no more strength to cry out to You Abba; My throat is dry; My eyes grow dim while I wait on You Abba, My redeemer;

Psalm 69

They that hate and seek to destroy Me for no reason, seem innumerable; they are mighty against Me, blinded to the truth that I am not their enemy: in Me will You restore sight to those whom death has blinded;

O Abba, You know the folly of men's hearts and their sin is not hid from You; that You might destroy it;

Let not those that trust in You Abba; ever be ashamed for My name sake; let not those who see My testimony and call upon Your name ever be disappointed; O Abba;

For Your name's sake have I borne their shame; trusting in Your promise to clothe Me with life Abba; while standing naked in the face of the enemy; death;

They treated Me as one in whom they had no friendship or regard; even My mother's children disowned Me;

Your passionate desire to clothe upon Me and all Your beloved Your life and immortality has consumed Me; and the shame of those in death; laboring to be clothed upon with life by their works; their grief, sorrow and shame toward You Abba, have fallen upon Me;

When I cried out to You Abba in My affliction; not considering My own ability to save Myself from death; they considered Me, smitten of You Abba;

Making nothing of My ability to clothe Myself with life and immortality; My testimony has become the Word for all people;

Those who placed their trust in their own works; did speak against Me and judged Me as forsaken; and the drunkards mocked Me in song;

But as for Me; My cry and My prayer is to You, O Abba, You have heard My cry and in the fullness of time You answered; with an abundance of Your grace and truth; in My salvation;

Delivering Me from the pit that I sink not and perish; delivering Me from those that hated Me without cause, from the deep waters;

Letting not my heart be overflowed by troubles that they might swallow Me up, leaving Me not in the grave to perish or to see corruption;

You hear Me O Abba; for Your loving-kindness is only good; answering Me according to the greatness and abundance of Your tender mercy and grace;

Psalm 69

You hid not Your face from Me; but heard Me when I cried; in My affliction You heard and answered Me speedily;

Drawing nigh unto Me and My life to redeem it: delivering Me from death;

You have known My reproach and My shame; Those who stand firmly against Me as the way unto life are before You;

In My distress I was weak having lost all strength and I found no one who took pity or gave comfort to Me among them, to help Me;

Instead, they gave Me poison for My food saying "save Yourself"; and for My thirst they gave Me vinegar to drink instead of pure water;

Let the food they have been eating for life; which is the works of their own hands; become a snare before them: and the thing that they expect to bring them peace, let it become a trap;

A veil that darkens their eyes of understanding, that they see not; giving them up to despair; unable to find peace in their flesh;

Pour out Your wrath upon all that which is contrary to Your life, and let Your wrathful anger take hold of it to destroy it;

Making its house desolate; with no one left to dwell in it;

For they that persecute and reject the One who bore our griefs and our sorrows; mock the One who was wounded for our transgression;

They will add iniquity to their iniquity: not allowing themselves to come to You for life; having condemned themselves;

For those who love not Your life will be blotted out of the book of the living; and not written with the righteous;

But I am poor in spirit; let Your salvation; O Abba, be revealed in raising Me up and setting Me at Your right hand;

I have praised and spoken well of Your name Abba; by calling upon Your name; with song and thanksgiving;

This is the offering that pleases You Abba; better than ox or bulls;

Those with no ability to give themselves life, will see it and rejoice and be glad; causing their hearts to rest in the life and immortality You revealed in Me; Abba;

For You Abba hear the cry of those who call upon Your name; and He will despise not those who trust in My testimony;

Let heaven and earth be joined in praise of Him and everything that moves therein;

For Abba will save from death all those who call upon His name; raising them up from corruption; that they may dwell in the house of the Lord forever; coheirs of His life as their possession;

All who find their testimony in Me, the Son; shall possess the same life and immortality as their inheritance; and they that love His life will dwell in Him and He in them and He will forever be with them.

Psalm 70

Make haste, O Abba to save and deliver Me; make haste to help Me in My trouble;

Let all that seeks to hurt and destroy Me and any of Your beloved be made desolate, and all those who seek to destroy My life be turned back from their way;

Let those who rejoice in iniquities reward be turned back in disappointment; those who wag their heads at Me, rejoicing in evil;

Let all those that seek You be glad and rejoice in You, never being disappointed; and let those who love Your life and salvation constantly magnify Your name Abba;

But I am poor in spirit, not possessing the ability to clothe upon myself with Your life and immortality: make haste unto Me, O Abba: You are My helper and My deliverer; O Abba My Lord, make no delay.

Psalm 71

In You O Abba, do I find My rest; In You will I never be disappointed or ashamed;

You deliver Me, safely hiding Me inside Your incorruptible life; where there is freedom from the sting of the death and corruption that is in the world; always inclining Your ear to Me; to save Me;

You are My strong refuge; where I continually find rest; You have promised to save Me; for You Abba are My mighty fortress, My firm foundation, My strength, My shield and My defender;

Psalm 71

You deliver Me, O Abba, from the wickedness that is in the world through death; and from the cruelty of those animated by it;

For You are My hope, O Abba, My Lord and My shepherd; You are My rest from My youth.

By You was I nurtured and sustained from the womb; You art He that severed Me from My mother's womb and set Me apart unto Your life; to reveal You Abba; speaking well of You continually;

I am a sign and a wonder to those who are suffering at the hands of death; testifying of You as My only hope and refuge;

Let My word and My testimony be filled with Your praise; continually speaking well and honoring You;

You do not cast Me away in My old age; or forsake Me when death surrounds Me and I have no strength;

And My enemies speak against Me; and they take counsel against Me;

Saying together that You Abba have forsaken Me; and that there is none to save Me;

O Abba; be not far from Me; O My God; make haste to save Me in My affliction;

Let all that seek to harm Me be confounded and their ways brought to nothing; and let the way that brought destruction to all Your beloved; collapse under its own weight when Your life is revealed;

I will only hope in You continually and speak well of You more and more;

My testimony shall speak an eternal word revealing the awesome wonders of Your indestructible life and Your salvation, putting it on display in Me, for all to see; for man knows not the depths thereof;

I will go forth in Your strength and not My own Abba; I will speak of Your promise of life to all people; for there is only life in You;

Abba, You have taught Me from My youth; and from that time have I declared Your wonderful works;

Now also when I am old and death tries to come to Me; it has nothing in Me; For My life is hid inside Your life O Abba; and You will never leave or forsake Me; My testimony shows forth Your strength and salvation to this generation and all those to come;

O Abba; In Your strength and ability to save Me from death and raise Me to Your life and immortality; exalting Me to Your right hand; You have done a marvelous work; O Abba, there is none like You;

You saw Me in My affliction; and when I cried You heard Me and quicken Me again; You brought Me up again from the grave;

You increased My greatness; and comforted Me on every side as a testimony for all people;

In Me; You are spoken well of in all the earth; declaring Your grace and truth; O Abba; You have spoken well of all people in Me; putting a new song in their hearts; setting Me apart; the Holy One of Israel; in whom You dwell with the power of an endless life in immortal flesh;

You cause My lips to sing praises unto Your name; and My life which You have redeemed to rejoice;

The word You have spoken and which was made immortal flesh in Me, has revealed Your life and immortality to all people; for You have confounded the logic and consumed the death that sought to destroy Your beloved.

Psalm 72

O Abba, My God and My King, You have given Me Your judgments; revealing Your life and immortality, in and through Me Your son;

Declaring Your justice for all people by the life revealed in Me; in immortal flesh in My resurrection; and to those who see they have no ability to clothe themselves with life, Your judgment to give them the kingdom as a gift;

Your judgments bring peace to Your people and assurance to their hearts by the life revealed in Me in immortal flesh and bone;

Bringing justice to those who do not look to their own ability but rest in You Abba; to save them from the death that has oppressed them;

They shall worship You until the moon and the sun pass away; throughout all generations;

You shall pour out Your Spirit upon all flesh; like rain that covers the earth;

I shall reign at Your right hand, Abba; bringing an abundance of peace on earth until the heavens be no more;

My dominion shall be from sea to sea, and over all the earth;

They that abide as strangers in dry land shall see Me and bow down; and sin and death will bend its knee to My dominion;

Psalm 72

Distant kings shall pay tribute; offering gifts;

And all the kings of the earth shall fall down before Me; and people from every tongue and every nation will worship Me; Your name's sake;

For in Me; shall You deliver those who cry out to You in their affliction; and also those who look to You Abba, seeing that they possess no ability to save themselves;

You shall save to the uttermost those who see they have no ability and those who cry out in their weakness; saving their life from destruction;

In Me Abba; You shall redeem their life from death and from the lies that have brought fear and torment to their hearts; their lives are precious in Your sight;

And they shall find their life in Me; who reigns at Your right hand; in whom all Your glory has been given; who continually makes intercession in their hearts; and daily will they see My life and My testimony; the word Abba, that You have spoken in Me has spoken well of them;

Abba, in Me, You have brought an abundance of meat into the storehouse; by seating Me at Your right hand; the fruit of My life shall be like a wave and peace offering; And they, that abide in My life and My testimony, shall prosper like the grass upon the earth;

You have given Me a name that shall endure forever; and people from every tongue and every nation shall call Me blessed forevermore;

I have spoken well of You Abba; the God of Israel; You have done wondrous things in and through Me;

You have spoken well of and glorified Me, Your name sake; forever; Abba; now also let the whole earth be glorified immortal; Amen and Amen.

These are Your words and Your prayers for Me, Abba.

www.ingramcontent.com/pod-product-compliance
Lightning Source LLC
Chambersburg PA
CBHW070759050426
42452CB00012B/2401